Sharks

SHARKS

BY RHODA BLUMBERG

FRANKLIN WATTS
NEW YORK | LONDON | 1976

Photographs courtesy of:

Marineland of Florida: frontispiece, pp. 3, 4, 9, 10, 20, 32, 38, 43, 46 (bottom), 52, 53, 65; New York Zoological Society: pp. 15, 44, 46 (top); Australian Information Service: pp. 25, 54; Texas Parks and Wildlife Department: p. 30; The American Museum of Natural History: pp. 31, 58, 59; The National Audubon Society Collection, Photo Researchers, Inc.: p. 35; Elgin Ciampi: p. 62; National Marine Fisheries Service: p. 63.

Library of Congress Cataloging in Publication Data

Blumberg, Rhoda.
    Sharks.

    (A First book)
    Bibliography: p.
    Includes index.
    SUMMARY: Introduces the physical characteristics, habits, and natural environment of different varieties of sharks.
    1. Sharks—Juvenile literature. [1. Sharks] I. Title.
QL638.9.B56   597′.31   75-45120
ISBN 0-531-00846-0

Contents

Sharks

Meet the Shark

Most of us think of sharks as great monsters whose sharp fins split the surface of the water as they race to kill. There are such sharks, but there are many other kinds as well.

About three hundred kinds, or **species,** of sharks have been found so far, and new ones are still being discovered. Full-grown sharks come in all sizes, from slightly over four inches to sixty feet long.

There are more shapes than you can imagine. Picture one with a mouth six feet wide that is crammed with thousands of teeth. How would you like to see a shark whose eyes and nostrils are a yard apart, or one with a long nose that looks like a sharp saw? Would you want to be face to face with a creature whose head is shaped like a shovel, or would you rather see one that looks like a giant snake?

Although most sharks are found in warm salt waters, some live under the ice in the north, and others swim in fresh water lakes and rivers all over the world. Some sharks live in shallow waters, near the shore. Most of the others are hidden by the vastness of the ocean, some swimming near the surface, others living as much as two miles below the surface.

(1)

Sharks have always frightened people by their fierce and sudden attacks — attacks that make them seem like mindless eating machines. Sharks are unpredictable; no one can tell what they will do. Seeming to be curious and harmless, they may approach a diver, only to attack viciously. And then there are instances of sharks fleeing from people, as though afraid.

Sailors have been terrified by sharks following their ships. Attracted by garbage thrown overboard, these fish seem ready to eat whatever might land in the sea. Many a shipwrecked sailor has seen his shipmates eaten by sharks.

Some people who must earn their living from the sea have fought their fear of sharks in different ways. Japanese fishermen wore red sashes to protect them from sea monsters. For the same reason, pearl divers in Ceylon sought the magic powers of shark charmers. The natives of the Fiji Islands performed a shark-kissing ceremony. After sharks were caught in nets, appointed "shark-kissers" waded out and kissed the sharks' bellies. This was supposed to make all sharks friendly.

Fear of sharks has caused people to worship them as gods, and to offer human sacrifices to them. In an effort to

The jagged teeth in this sand tiger shark's mouth will finish off its victim very quickly.

MARINELAND OF FLORIDA

A primitive monster that has survived millions of
years, this sand tiger shark searches the seas for food.

satisfy sharks, some coastal tribes in Africa tied people to stakes in shallow water, where sharks could devour them. To honor the Hawaiian shark god, Kama-Hoa-Lii, an ancient ruler built a walled circle in shallow water, with a gate to the open sea. This was a sea theater for shark fights, where men, armed with daggers made of sharks' teeth, fought man-eating sharks. The king and his people watched the bloody show from the safety of the shore.

Others had a better way of soothing their sharks. Solomon Islanders threw pig meat into the sea. Tahitians built temples where they prayed and called the shark their protector and friend. And in the New Hebrides the body of a dead shark was placed on an altar, where it was decorated and worshiped.

Sharks have been in the seas for more than 300 million years. We know this because scientists have found impressions of a shark's body and skin in rocks that old. An ancient shark had pressed against mud that turned to stone. These rocks were found along the banks of a river near Cleveland, Ohio.

Sharks' teeth found in rocks tell scientists about the types of sharks that lived long ago. Many sharks that lived millions of years ago were like the ones we find today. Although sharks have tiny brains, and are said to have little intelligence, they are skilled at surviving, and they have lived on while dinosaurs and other great monsters of the past have disappeared. They have survived because of their strong bodies and their ability to hunt and to kill. A **primitive** monster is alive and with us still.

The Shark's Body

The shark doesn't have a bone in its body. Instead of bones, its skeleton is made of **cartilage**. Cartilage is found in the hard, bendable part of your ears and nose. Sharks, skates, and rays are called cartilaginous fish. All other fishes have bones and are called bony fishes. Although the shark does not have a backbone, like most fishes, it does have a spinal column. It is called a **vertebrate**.

A shark's skin is different, too. Instead of scales, the skin has thousands of teeth — tiny sharp points covered with hard **enamel**. These skin teeth, called **dermal denticles**, make the skin so rough that carpenters have used shark skin instead of sandpaper to polish wood.

Most fish have air bladders, sacs of gas inside their bodies that make them lighter than water. The air bladder acts like a balloon. It helps them float. Since sharks don't have air bladders, they must swim continually or they will sink, because they are heavier than water. In some sharks, however, the liver offers some help. It is large and full of oil, and since oil is lighter than water, it helps keep the shark afloat.

Sharks are doomed to keep on the move for another

reason. If they stop swimming, they will stop breathing.

To breathe, all fishes need **gills,** which enable them to remove oxygen from water. Bony fishes use their mouths as pumps, opening and closing them to force water back to their gills. Even though sharks have from five to seven gills on each side of their heads, they have a special problem breathing. Most sharks can't pump water. Instead, they must keep swimming to force water into their gills. They swim with their mouths open. Water then rushes through their mouths into their gills, and they can breathe. They may doze at times, swimming while sleeping.

Because they must be on the move in order to live and keep afloat, nature has supplied the shark with a strong tail and strong **fins**. A powerful tail whose upper fin is larger than the lower fin sweeps back and forth, propelling the shark forward. Two large fins near the head are held out like wings to balance the body. The fins are stiff. The shark cannot fold them back against its body the way bony fishes do with their fins. A set of rear fins and a fin on the belly help the shark move swiftly. The streamlined, torpedo shape typical of most sharks also helps its body glide through the water.

Although their average speed is three to five miles per hour, sharks have been known to race along at over forty miles an hour. They can speed in short spurts, when they are chasing food or fleeing from an enemy. However, they can't stop quickly, and they are not able to back up. Instead, their boneless bodies must bend and curve to turn back.

JAWS

Sharks have the most powerful jaws in the world. The jaw-power of an eight-foot shark was measured on a bite meter, a metal scale wrapped inside bait. The bite pressure was eighteen tons per square inch! It is no wonder that sharks have bent propellers and made holes in boats with their jaws.

Sharks have teeth of all shapes and sizes. Some sharks have teeth several inches long, razor-sharp for cutting. Others have jagged teeth, for tearing. And there are flat teeth, used for crushing shells and bones. Some sharks have sharp teeth in front and crushing teeth in back.

Scientists are usually able to name the type of shark by the type of tooth. A triangular tooth with jagged edges could be that of a white shark; large, pointed fangs could be those of a blue pointer; a ragged tooth, that of a sand shark; a tiny pinlike spike could have been lost by a whale shark. The Florida Indians used to look for shark teeth. They used them for arrowheads — and they didn't need to sharpen them.

Because the teeth are not set in a jawbone, sharks lose them often. All sharks have extra teeth in their jaws to replace the ones that come out, or wear out. Most sharks have rows of teeth, one behind the other. Five or six rows are usual. Except for the front teeth, others lie flat, like shingles on a roof, one behind the other. When a front tooth is lost, a back one springs up, moves forward, and takes its place. Also, as a shark grows, larger teeth replace smaller ones. A shark can use up more than 20,000 teeth in ten years. That shouldn't be too amazing, since

These ragged teeth belong to a sand tiger shark.
Developing teeth in the inner rows
lie in reserve, waiting to replace lost outer teeth.

(9)

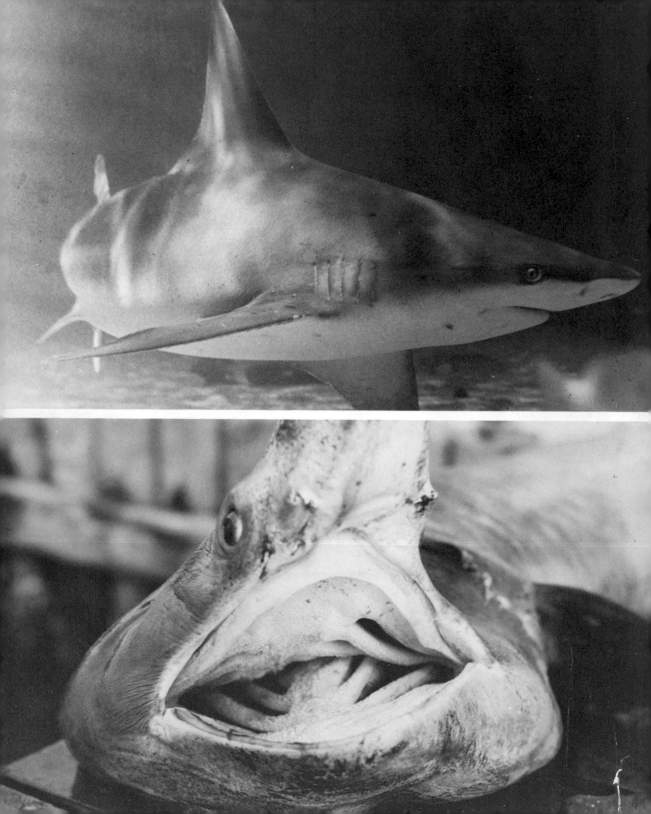

some shark mouths have 3,000 teeth in use at one time.

Although they can bite chunks of food, lots of sharks are "gulpers." The great white shark can swallow whole something half its own size. When one fifteen-footer was opened up, the bodies of two six-foot sharks were found inside its stomach.

The largest sharks eat the smallest pieces of food. Whale sharks and basking sharks swim lazily at two or three miles an hour, holding their giant mouths wide open. Tons of water carrying food flow through their jaws. Inside their mouths, **gill rakers** act as strainers. The rakers keep food in the shark's mouth, allowing the strained water to pass on through the gills. The basking shark has over one thousand stiff rakers, which look like bristles. The whale shark has spongy tissue, between bars of cartilage, which strains the water and traps food in its mouth.

Whale sharks and basking sharks are called filter feeders. Their main diet is **plankton** — floating masses of tiny plants and animals. A basking shark twenty-three feet long can strain 4 million pounds of sea water in one hour. No one has figured out how much a sixty-foot whale shark could wash into its six-foot jaws.

Above: this sandbar shark has five gills on each side of its head. Below: the mouth of this basking shark is filled with stiff, bristle-like gill rakers that strain its food from the water that constantly flows through its jaws.

The Shark Hunts for Food

The hungry shark must find food. The shark's ability to hear, smell, see, taste, and touch leads it to its prey.

HEARING

A shark's hearing is excellent. Sounds may be the first clue that dinner is somewhere in the water. The famous sea explorer Jacques Cousteau tested the shark's sense of hearing. He noted that sharks hear clapping, bells, and the noise divers make. Sometimes Cousteau made noises just to attract them to his underwater cameras. To be safe, the cameramen locked themselves in metal cages below the surface. Sharks came to look at the human zoo with its collection of people behind bars.

SMELLING

Sharks have a keen sense of smell. They have been called hounds of the sea because they are able to follow a scent when they hunt. Their brains have been described as smelling organs because two thirds of the brain's weight is used for smelling. The nostrils are never used for breathing but for picking up odors of fish, animals, and plants. Since a shark is able to detect one part of blood to 100 million parts of water, it is no surprise that a tiny drop of blood can attract sharks from a quarter of a mile away. Wounded prey brings them quickly, but sharks can also follow the scent of healthy fish.

SEEING

Until a few years ago, it was believed that sharks didn't see very well. Experiments have shown that they can see objects one hundred feet away.

Sharks may not be able to see color, but they can see patterns, such as stripes and crosses. Their eyes can be tiny, or bigger than your fist. They glow in the dark. Most sharks have eyelids. Some sharks have an extra eyelid, a thin white skin that slides over the eyes just before a shark attacks. Tales have been told about the wicked wink of sharks whose black eyes turn dead white. And there are reports of sharks who lift their heads out of the water to peer into a boat.

FEELING

All fish can sense moving bodies without seeing them. Through **pressure waves,** fish are able to tell the speed, size, and form of an object. Like all other fish, sharks have a narrow band of nerves on each side, from their eyes to their tails. This is the **lateral line**. It picks up motions in the water made by fish and animals nearby. The lateral line has been called a sense of distant touch, and a direction finder, for it tells fish through waves and water currents how deep the water is, and where other fish and animals are swimming.

TASTING AND TOUCHING

Once sharks hear, smell, see, or sense their victims, they close in for the kill. Sharks circle around the fish or animal about to be eaten. They keep making their circles smaller and smaller until they bump against their victim. They bump to feel their prey, and in so doing sometimes stun it. Sharks have **pit organs** all over their bodies. Scientists thought these were taste buds. We now know that the pit organs just enable sharks to feel whatever they touch.

A shark has taste buds in its mouth, in its throat, and on its tongue. Experiments prove that sharks prefer the taste of certain foods. Some, for example, prefer tuna. Others prefer the taste of turtle.

After the bump comes the bite. Although their mouths are underneath their snouts, sharks do not have to roll over on their backs to bite, but can raise their snouts up in the air. Their jaws jut out. Some sharks have teeth that tip

This nurse shark's boneless body bends and curves as it turns.

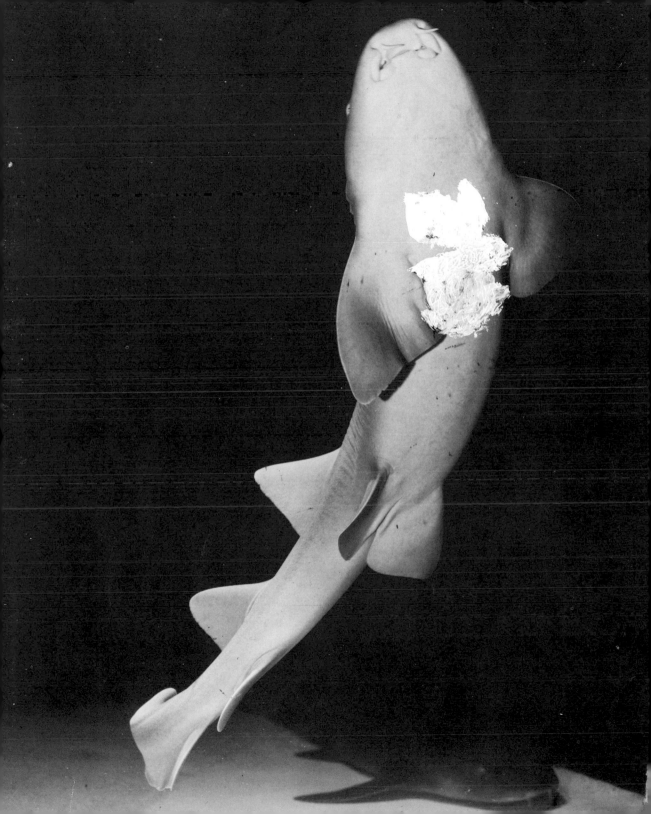

forward when their jaws open. They lock into an upright position until the jaws snap shut. Then the teeth tip back again.

THE FEEDING FRENZY

Sometimes hundreds of large sharks come from all directions to attack the same victim. They crowd together in a mad mob scene. Whalers have watched bodies of dead whales being stripped of all flesh as hundreds of sharks feast. The sea seems to boil over as the sharks thrash about, and the water turns red with blood.

The sharks lose all control. They become mindless eating machines, so excited that they bite and eat and tear at anything near them. They slam their jaws at anchors, chains of ships — whatever is in the water. They eat each other, and while bending and turning they sometimes bite and feed on their own bodies. They become numb to pain. This insane jaw-snapping at anything is called **feeding frenzy.** It has been seen only among big sharks, such as blue sharks and whitetip sharks.

It is interesting that the same sharks that go crazy filling their stomachs can go without food for weeks. The oil stored in their livers keeps them going. We still do not know when they are going to attack to feed, and when and why they stop eating for long periods of time.

Although sharks can preserve food in their stomachs for a long time, they can **digest** very rapidly. A large shark was caught with the tail of a hammerhead still in its jaws, while the head had already been digested in the stomach.

ODDS AND ENDS
IN THE
SHARK'S STOMACH

Sharks may bite at anything. They sometimes swallow things they cannot digest. These stay inside their stomachs until the stomach lining turns itself inside out in the mouth and dumps everything out, or until people cut sharks open. Then some surprising items come out.

A shark caught near Australia had swallowed a whole goat, a large turtle, a cat, three birds, and some fish, including another shark six feet long. Four coats and a car license plate were taken from a shark that once swam near Italy. Nine pairs of shoes and some belts and pants found their way into the stomach of a shark from the Philippines. A northern shark swallowed a reindeer. A few hundred years ago the headless body of a knight in armor came out of a shark's belly.

In 1799 James Briggs, an American sea captain, was sentenced to jail because of papers found inside a shark. His ship, the *Nancy,* had been trading with the French, who were Britain's enemies at that time.

Just before he was captured in the Caribbean, he threw a bundle of his papers overboard, so that there would be no proof that he was dealing with the French. A British ship docked at Jamaica. Its crew had caught a large shark, cut it open, and found the papers in such good condition that they could be read in court. Captain Briggs was proven guilty of crimes against Britain. The original "Shark Papers" are now on display in Jamaica.

The Shark's Companions

Who would think that any fish would choose to swim around with sharks? Yet there are some little fish who like to travel with them, and with other big fish. The pilot fish and the suckerfish like the shark's company.

PILOT FISH

Pilot fish catch the crumbs of food that slip out of a shark's jaws. They get free meals and safety, because the pilot's enemies steer clear of their giant table mates. Pilot fish stay near all kinds of sharks.

They are beautiful creatures, no longer than two feet. They look like a colorful honor guard for the shark. Some have blue stripes. Others, called sergeant majors, are black and yellow.

At one time, people believed that these fish really acted as pilots for sharks, who were supposed to have such poor eyesight. That is the reason for their name. Now we know that pilots just stay around for an easy meal. They don't do anything for the shark, and if their host is not eating too well, they swim off and find another shark or big fish who will supply them with better meals. They seem to stay away from a shark's mouth, so that they don't end up in its stomach.

SUCKERFISH

Remoras, known as suckerfish, are also the shark's companions. Like pilot fish, they have their meals with their big hosts. But they don't even have to swim along. They make themselves at home on the shark and get a free ride.

Suckerfish are the hitchhikers of the ocean world. They ride along for food and lodging. The shark is really stuck, for the suckerfish has an oval pad of suckers on top of its head that makes it stick fast to a shark's skin. Suckerfish range in size from a few inches to three feet. Some are red, others gray or green. Suckers don't depend entirely on leftovers from a shark's meal. They often pull themselves off and catch their own food. Then they return to the shark's body or find another large host.

Suckers like to eat copepods — little shellfish that dig into a shark's skin. So when suckers clean house by eating these copepods, they are getting rid of pests that bother sharks.

Although pilot fish do nothing for the shark, the suckerfish perform a valuable service. But sharks do not appreciate them. Suckers must watch out, depending for safety on their own speed and agility. They, like pilot fish, are gobbled up by the shark if they are not wary.

Two remoras accompany
this sand tiger shark.

(20)

Suckerfish attach themselves to many kinds of big fish and to turtles. They also stick to the bottoms of boats. Indians in the Caribbean used them for bait to catch turtles because of their sucking power. Columbus saw how this was done. The Indians gathered suckers that clung to their canoe bottoms. They attached their lines to the live suckers and cast them into the sea. The suckers glued themselves to large turtles. Then the Indians pulled in their catch.

People in the West Indies, China, Australia, and Africa still use suckerfish as bait. Being hitchhiker of the sea is not all easy or safe.

The Shark's Enemies

Sharks do not have many enemies, and most living things flee in terror from them. But there are a few enemies that can hurt and even kill sharks.

We are still learning about the feeding habits of sea creatures. We know that giant squids have devoured sharks. So have alligators and crocodiles when sharks swim near the mouths of rivers. Swordfish slash at sharks in self-defense, but don't usually win their duels. Killer whales prey on sharks. A killer whale was seen off the coast of California with a nine-foot shark in its mouth. The whale leaped out of the water and held the shark high before starting its meal.

SHARKS

The shark's most common foe is another shark. Big sharks eat smaller sharks. Strong ones eat weaker ones. And they will eat their own species. Hammerheads eat hammerheads; tiger sharks eat other tiger sharks. Mako shark mothers have been seen eating their young. Sometimes one shark swallows another that has been hooked by a fisherman. One shark on the hook is swallowed by a second shark, who is then hooked.

Sharks are able to judge the size of other fish with amazing accuracy. A shark called the smooth dogfish knows that it must avoid another smooth dogfish only 7 percent larger. Sharks of different sizes avoid each other. Those swimming together are all the same size, feeling safe as long as they are away from larger sharks.

PORCUPINE FISH

A porcupine fish that starts out as food for a shark can end up by killing it. The largest porcupine fish is three feet long. Its skin is covered with sharp spikes, and it is a "puffer." It blows itself up like a balloon when it is inside its enemy's mouth. Then its spikes dig into the shark's throat and choke it to death.

PORPOISES

Porpoises have battled sharks and killed them. They attack to protect themselves, because shark meat is not their natural food. But porpoise flesh is one of the shark's foods.

Porpoises live in groups, always ready to protect their babies. Any shark who grabs a young porpoise is in for trouble. The grown-ups in the group use their heads to ram the shark. They crash at top speed, with their heads hitting into the shark. They slam into its stomach, ripping apart the shark's insides. Or they choose the shark's gills as their target and destroy its ability to breathe.

Porpoises and sharks have also been seen swimming peacefully together in the ocean. In one aquarium, porpoises and a shark were put together in the same pool. All went well until a few days before a female porpoise gave birth. Then the porpoises used teamwork. They zoomed in full-speed against the shark and killed it. They seemed to know that a baby porpoise would end up in the shark's stomach.

PEOPLE

People kill millions of sharks each year. We are their deadly enemy.

Sportsmen enjoy catching some kinds of sharks because they are battlers, and there are plenty of them in the sea. Seeing a hooked mako shark leap fifteen feet out of the water can be exciting to a fisherman.

After the movie *Jaws* stirred up mass hatred of sharks, so-called monster boats became popular. The skippers took people out, not for the sport of fishing, but to have customers kill sharks, as though sharks were the enemy. How senseless, for sharks are neither evil nor bloodthirsty. Like other fish, they just hunt to survive.

This 3,234-pound great white shark was caught off the coast of Western Australia.

Divine Child Elementary
Dearborn, Mich.

Shark fishing has been big business for a long time. Shark liver oil was used to light up lamps. This oil was also taken by the spoonful because it is rich in vitamin A. Now vitamin A is made with chemicals, a cheaper, easier way.

Shark skin, called **shagreen,** has been made into leather goods, like shoes, belts, and handbags. Gift shops sell bracelets and necklaces made of shark teeth, and jaws are sold as wall decorations. Shark flesh has been ground for fertilizer and pet food. And now shark meat is sold in many fish markets.

The soupfin shark wouldn't enjoy knowing its name, because when caught it is fated to have its fins in a boiling pot. Soupfin shark becomes sharkfin soup, a popular Chinese dish. In Japan, sharks have always been a favorite food, especially *kamaboko,* shark fish cakes. The fish in the well-known fish and chips served in England and Australia is often shark.

Our own fish markets sell small sharks called dogfish as "grayfish." Mako shark is becoming very popular and can be ordered in many restaurants. There is one great advantage to eating shark. You don't have to worry about swallowing a bone.

The Facts of Life

Usually sharks have their babies in a different way from that of most fish. Most fish lay an enormous number of eggs. A haddock, for example, can lay 3 million, and a codfish is able to lay 9 million eggs at one time. These eggs, usually laid in water, are fertilized by the male fish when he pours his seed called **sperm** over them.

If all these eggs became fish, the oceans would be packed as tight as a sardine can. But only a small percentage of the eggs hatch. The rest are eaten by fish, or just drift into water too cold or too warm for them to hatch.

MATING

Sharks, too, have eggs. However, all shark eggs are fertilized inside the mother's body. Male sharks mate with female sharks. Each male has two sex organs, or **claspers.** They are called claspers because people once thought they were used to clasp, or hold on to, the female during mating. We now know that males usually hold on to their mates with their teeth! The claspers send sperm inside the female and fertilize the eggs.

(27)

In many species of shark, adult males travel together, separated from females. They just visit the opposite sex during mating season, which for many sharks takes place in the spring or summer.

Not very much is known about male courtship behavior. We do know that the males stop eating. They are nourished by the oil in their livers until mating is finished. Some scientists think that their lack of appetite protects the female. But the female is well able to take care of herself. Although she may come away with teeth marks from her mate, she is bigger than he. She could attack and kill him. Whether this ever happens, we don't know, but some scientists suspect that it occurs. That may explain why there are more adult females than males in some species.

Pregnant females usually keep to themselves until they are ready to give birth at their breeding grounds. Some pick shallow waters, and others give birth at the bottom of the sea. Males rarely come to the area.

SHARK EGGS

Although eggs are always fertilized inside the female, a few sharks lay their eggs in water. You might find shark eggs washed up on beaches. Their shells are thick and rubbery. Called witches' purses or mermaids' purses, they feel like leather. They come in yellow, black, or brown, and in many shapes and sizes. The eggs have sticky, threadlike **tendrils** that act as anchors. The tendrils stick to rocks or seaweed, trying to hold the eggs in one place until hatching time.

Each kind of shark has its own type of egg. The five-inch shell of a horn shark, shaped like a twisted cone, has tendrils seven feet long. The egg case of a cat shark looks like a leather bag with strings on the corners. The whale shark, the biggest shark of all, is an egg layer. An egg washed ashore measured twenty-seven inches long by sixteen inches wide.

Most of these eggs hatch after six months, but some take as long as fifteen months to open. After the fish inside the egg grows to a certain size, the witch's purse opens slightly to let in seawater. Then the unborn shark can swim in the egg, until the shell finally breaks open.

BEARING PUPS

The eggs of most kinds of sharks hatch inside the mother's body, and the sharks are born live, looking and acting like tiny adults. Before birth some species develop by feeding first on the egg's yolk. Then a cord forms, attaching the unborn shark to its mother, and its mother's bloodstream supplies the nourishment.

In most species, unborn sharks do not grow a cord connecting them with their mothers. After they feed on the yolks of their own eggs, their eggs hatch and they devour other eggs inside their mother. At least one kind of shark is a **cannibal** before it is born. The unborn sand tiger shark will eat up its brothers and sisters as they hatch inside.

Newborn sharks are called **pups.** Sharks have between two and one hundred young at one time. This is a

Baby whale shark and egg case.
Whale sharks average thirty-five feet or
more in length when fully grown.

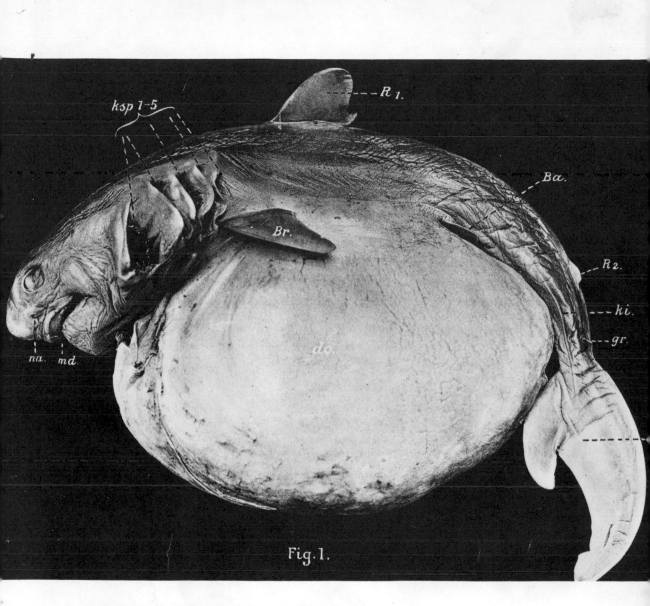

Fig. 1.

Egg with embryo of the mackerel shark

small number compared with the millions of young hatched by bony fishes.

When the female arrives at the breeding grounds, sometimes after a very long journey, she loses her desire for food. That protects the new pups from being eaten by her. Shortly after giving birth, she leaves, free to travel and eat again.

GROWING UP

When the mother goes away, the breeding grounds become a nursery with no grown-ups in charge. After a short time the young sharks leave their nursery and travel out into the watery world together. Males and females do not go their separate ways until they are grown-up. Until then they swim near each other, away from adults who might devour them. They stay together until they are fully grown. Then the males usually leave the females, until they meet for mating. And the life cycle starts all over again.

The sand tiger is one of the species of sharks that are born live.

The Big Three

Although these three kinds of sharks are not seen too often, when one appears it makes big news. Two of these sharks are quite harmless. The third is the nightmare of the sea.

WHALE SHARK

There are whale sharks sixty feet long. That's as long as a bowling alley. Some scientists believe bigger ones may be hidden in the ocean. Most whale sharks average thirty-five feet long and weigh about ten tons, large enough to make anyone feel pretty small.

Whale sharks usually stay in tropical waters all over the world, but occasionally they stray as far north as Long Island, New York during summer. Because they are filter feeders, whale sharks keep their mouths open so that plankton and small fish can flow in. Some with mouths six feet wide keep them open two feet high to catch food. About 3,000 teeth are inside these big mouth traps. Whale sharks swim slowly, at about two or three miles an hour.

**Whale sharks like this one are huge monsters
that usually cruise lazily in tropical waters.**

Yellow and white spots on a dark body, crisscrossed with ridges and lines, make them look like giant checkerboards.

Since they feed only on plankton, some swimmers and deep-sea divers feel safe climbing on top of them. One of Cousteau's divers had to hold on tight when a large shark he was riding at the surface suddenly dropped down 150 feet. It was **sounding.** Instead of swimming down at a slant, it dropped down like an elevator going from the fifteenth to the first floor.

Whale sharks have banged into boats and damaged them, possibly because they are bumbling and clumsy. They may not always be gentle giants.

BASKING SHARK

A basking shark is a real oil tanker. It can grow as long as forty-five feet, weigh seven tons, and can hold 600 gallons of oil in its liver. About two hundred years ago New Englanders found this oil useful for their lamps, and for making candles. This shark could be harpooned nearby in north Atlantic waters.

Sometimes three or four basking sharks swim in line one behind the other, the snout of one touching the tail of the shark in front. People have reported seeing a mammoth monster hundreds of feet long, because they saw the head of the shark first in line and the tail of the last. Hundreds of basking sharks have been seen swimming together. They swim in waters cooler than those chosen by the whale shark. They are never in tropical waters.

Like whale sharks, they are filter feeders. Some cruise along with a mouth opening that is three feet square. Baskers stay at the surface of the water, moving along lazily, and swimmers have enjoyed riding on them.

They don't always cruise along calmly. Sometimes they leap out of the water. One of these big, heavy giants was seen jumping so high that its tail was six feet above the water.

THE GREAT WHITE SHARK

The great white shark is also known by other names: white death, man-eater, and death shark. The names are well earned, for the great white shark is the most aggressive, most dangerous creature in the sea. It has killed more people than any other shark. No one knows when or why it should choose to attack.

The great white shark is sometimes all white, but it is also brown, blue, or gray. Only its belly is always white, like the underside of most sharks. Because of its pointed snout, it is also called blue pointer and white pointer. It can grow up to forty feet, but is usually not more than twenty-five feet long, weighing several tons.

Its jaws hold large, triangular-shaped teeth jagged as saws, able to cut through bones and flesh with one bite. The great white shark moves fast and attacks with terrifying speed. Shooting through the water, it travels like a torpedo. It sometimes goes after boats, damaging many and sinking some. Fish, sea turtles, smaller sharks, seals,

and even birds that land on the water may end up in its stomach. It is a garbage eater — a ship follower that eats anything thrown overboard.

This shark's stomach is so strong that it eats stingrays whose poison kills other fish. And the shark can swallow anything half its size with one gulp.

The great white shark lives in every ocean in the world and has been seen from Florida to Newfoundland, from southern California to Alaska. It goes north in the summer for cooler waters. Then it returns to the south in the winter. It usually swims alone. During its travels the great white shark sometimes comes near shore. That is frightening for people who enjoy beaches. Fortunately there are not many great white sharks, and they are rarely seen off North American shores.

One of the most dangerous killers of the sea — the great white shark

Well-known Sharks

The silent underworld of the sea has hardly been explored. The sharks we know best are the ones that come up to the surface, those caught by fishermen, and those found by undersea explorers. About three hundred kinds of sharks have been found so far.

BLUE SHARK

The blue shark is probably the most beautiful of all, with dark-blue back, brilliant blue sides, and a snow-white belly. Its slim body races gracefully through the waters. A seven-foot blue weighs only seventy pounds. Adults can be about twelve feet long.

There are many blue sharks in the sea, for one female ten feet long can produce a litter of fifty pups, all hatched inside her, each about one foot in length.

Blue sharks are also called blue whalers, for good reason. When a whale is killed, blue sharks frequently appear. Only too often fishermen watch a feeding frenzy from their whaling boats during which their prize catch is stripped to the bone by hundreds of blues.

Blue sharks are usually found swimming in groups. Sometimes, in summer, hundreds of them swim in New England waters, crowding each other, making a thickly packed mass.

WHITETIP SHARK

So named because its fins are tipped white, it is a surface swimmer that likes warm waters. Although its litter of about six pups is small, there are probably more whitetips in the oceans than any other large shark. Perhaps they are plentiful because they are hard to kill. They will keep attacking even when hit by bullets, unless a bullet hits the brain. Whitetips can grow to about thirteen feet, but an eight-foot one is considered large.

To test how a whitetip would act, Jacques Cousteau's crew threw a dummy overboard, dressed as a skin diver. A whitetip shark ripped it apart at once. That was proof enough for the crew. Whitetips could probably be deadly.

TIGER SHARK

Found all over the world in warm waters, anywhere from near shore to far out to sea, this shark is called a tiger because of its brown stripes on a gray body. These stripes fade as tigers become old. Tigers can be eighteen feet long.

They deserve their name because they attack viciously. Tiger sharks are the terror killers of the Pacific, probably attacking more Australians than any other shark.

They have attacked people standing in three feet of water. In fact, most of their attacks on people take place in shallow waters. Tigers are hated by fishermen because they so often tear fishnets and eat an entire catch.

THRESHER

How would you like to see a fish twenty feet long with a tail that makes up half the length of its body? The thresher has been called sea ape, singletail, and peacock shark. The thresher rounds up its prey by curving its tail so that small fish are walled in. Then it uses this enormous tail to slap schools of fish into its jaws.

The thresher often comes close to shore in search of small schools of fish. It may swim around in circles, leaping into the air, then falling back into the water, beating its tail. The result is that schools of tiny fish huddle together, trying to escape this wild-acting shark. When the fish are crowded together, the thresher darts among them and gobbles them up.

The thresher is not dangerous — unless you happen to be near the tail, which can swat like a baseball bat. It has only two or three pups in a litter, but each baby is about five feet long. Threshers are found throughout the world in temperate waters.

NURSE SHARK

The nurse shark is a bottom dweller that likes water so shallow that its fins sometimes stick out in the air. It often

The vicious tiger shark

(43)

hides in caves or under reefs in the sea. Slow and lazy, it doesn't move around very much. When it does, it swims like a snake. Winding back and forth, it inspects the floor of the sea for crabs, lobsters, and other food.

A nurse shark doesn't have to keep moving, because it pumps water over its gills. Skin divers have seen nurse sharks lying still side by side, like ships docked in port. They have clambered over their bodies without being harmed, but nurse sharks have attacked people for no apparent reason.

You can tell a nurse shark from other common sharks because it has **barbels** — feelers made of flesh. A barbel hanging on each side of its mouth looks like a droopy mustache. Nurse sharks are found in the Atlantic and Pacific. They are the only sharks in the Atlantic with barbels, and they can be fourteen feet long.

There are many explanations for the word *nurse*. Many believe the word was used because at one time people thought this shark carried its babies in its mouth. That's impossible, for the usual litter numbers twenty to thirty, and each pup is a foot long.

SAND SHARK

The sand shark is popular in aquariums. Its many rows of sharp, crooked teeth give it the horrible look that visitors

The nurse shark, with its distinctive barbels

(45)

Above: the sand shark spends its life almost
continuously swimming. Below: the mako, a favorite
of sportsmen, is generally a solitary swimmer.

(46)

seem to enjoy. The sand shark, also known as the ragged-tooth shark and the gray nurse shark, is a slow-moving fish that likes shallow waters. Found all over the world, it grows to ten feet in length and may weigh over 400 pounds, and it is dangerous.

Sand sharks can work as a team. Some hundred of them were seen herding a school of bluefish toward shore. The bluefish were trapped between land and sharks. Then the sand sharks ate them. There are sand sharks in North America that are not supposed to be dangerous. Sand sharks have, however, killed people off the shores of Africa and Australia.

MAKO SHARK

The mako is the sportsman's delight. A surface swimmer able to race at forty miles an hour, this swift and powerful fish puts up a hard fight. Once it is hooked, it can leap fifteen feet in the air trying to shake the hook out of its mouth. Imagine seeing a slim shark that may be twelve feet long, weighing 1,000 pounds, jumping so high. The mako has become a popular food. Some say its tasty flesh is due to its diet, which includes swordfish. One mako, weighing in at 720 pounds, had a 110-pound swordfish in its stomach, sword and all.

Makos will attack boats and people. Zane Grey, the famous author, described them as "death-dealing engines of the deep."

Sharks in Strange Places

Do you know that there are sharks that live and breed in freshwater lakes and rivers? Whoever pictured a shark swimming under the Arctic ice? Sharks show up in the strangest places.

ARCTIC SHARK

Eskimos cut holes in the ice to fish for the Arctic shark. They throw down lines with large hooks baited with fish. Once hooked, the shark is dragged back and forth in the water until it drowns. A shark drowns when it is pulled backward because it must swim forward all the time in order to breathe.

There is another way Eskimos catch sharks. They hold a fish bladder filled with blood over an ice hole. Then they let blood trickle into the water. When a shark shows up, attracted by the blood, they harpoon it.

Other names for the Arctic shark are Greenland shark and sleeper shark. The Arctic shark acts so sleepy that sometimes Eskimos just reach into the water and pull one out with their hands. They can do that with small sharks

— not the ones that grow to twenty-four feet long and weigh a ton.

Greenland Eskimos call anyone who is drunk "shark sick." That's because Arctic shark meat, if it is eaten raw, can make a person feel drunk or very sick. The Eskimos like raw fish, but they know that uncooked shark isn't good for them. By boiling shark meat they can eat it, and also feed it to their dogs without worrying about their pets becoming ill.

The Eskimos cut hair using shark's teeth as razors, and they also make strong ropes from the skin.

FRESHWATER SHARKS

Lake Nicaragua in Central America is teeming with man-eating sharks. Even its shallow waters can be dangerous. People have been attacked and killed close to the shores of this 110-mile-long freshwater lake.

Scientists have tried to explain how sharks came into the lake. Some say the lake was once connected with the Pacific Ocean. Others say that at one time there was an outlet from the lake to the Caribbean.

The Nicaragua shark is a puzzle for another reason. Although a river connects Lake Nicaragua with Lake Managua, no sharks have ever been seen in Lake Managua.

Lake Nicaragua is not the only body of freshwater with sharks. Lakes in Venezuela, Guatemala, New Guinea, and the Philippines have them. The same type of man-eater swims in the Ganges River in India. Religious pilgrims bathing in its holy waters have been attacked and killed. The Karun River in Iran, the Saigon River in Vietnam, and the Zambezi River in Africa have sharks, too. The deadly Zambezi shark lives at the mouth of its river, near the ocean, and also 340 miles up from the coast, enjoying the river's clear, sweet waters. There are freshwater sharks all over the world — even in rivers in Mississippi and Louisiana.

Several kinds of sharks enter rivers from the ocean. Hammerheads have wandered upstream. Certain sharks not yet identified have been seen in tropical rivers. These are usually small, about three feet long. But most sharks found in freshwater rivers and lakes are bull sharks. Bull sharks are heavyset fish that grow to ten feet long. They are as vicious as great white sharks.

Odd-looking Sharks

Hammers, saws, shovels, angels, goblins, and *dwarfs* are words that describe many strange sharks. Some are so queer-looking that they are like fairy-tale monsters.

HAMMERHEAD

There is more chance of seeing a hammerhead than any other strange shark. It is found all over the world, mostly near the shore. A hammerhead looks like an ordinary shark — except for its head. The head, shaped like a long pole, is at right angles to its body. Its eyes bulge at both ends of the pole, and its nostrils are near its eyes. A hammerhead can grow to fifteen feet long, and its head can be a yard wide. The head looks as though it has been hammered into a long, flat bar.

The common hammerhead hunts in packs and is dangerous to people as well as other hammerheads and fish. There are nine kinds of hammerheads. Small and large, they are equally dangerous. One kind has a head so round that it is called a bonnethead or shovelnose shark.

**A diver studies a
hammerhead shark.**

**This baby hammerhead is a
miniature of its parents.**

OTHER
ODD-LOOKING
SHARKS

Let's go from hammers and shovels to saws. There's a saw shark with a long, flattened snout that looks just like a saw, and is just as sharp. Sharp teeth stick out along its edges. The saw shark strikes and cuts its food with this strange snout. Luckily, saw sharks are not interested in people. They are found in the Far East and near Africa.

Wobbegong is an odd name well suited to a very odd shark. This shark looks like a big blob of flesh that has splashed and spilled on the ocean floor. Its fat, ugly head and the edges of its round speckled body have lots of barbels that look like whiskers. It likes to sleep in caves under the sea, and it crawls along the sea floor looking for food. The wobbegong, an Australian oddity, grows up to six feet in length. Its sharp teeth have dug into skin divers.

The "wobby" is a member of the carpet shark family. Some carpet sharks are as beautifully colored as Oriental rugs. But the common Australian wobbegong is a dull brown and beige — not the most attractive of carpets.

The patterned skins of some carpet sharks are often used in the shark leather industry. This shark also has numerous barbels.

The frilled shark, with its neck that looks like a fancy frilled collar, is another sight to see. It looks more like a snake than a shark, with its long, skinny body and snake-like head. It can be five feet long and four inches around.

The porbeagle shark is an oddity because of its deep-green eyes.

There's a swell shark that blows itself up like a balloon when it is in danger. It gulps water, and sometimes air. Then it floats on the surface, belly up, away from its enemy. The swell shark is common off the coast of southern California.

The spiny dogfish shark has poison spines all over its skin. When it attacks, it curves its body into a bow and lunges forward with the spines sticking out. It is found in European and American waters.

Midget sharks include a nine-incher called a dwarf shark, and one between four and five inches long, the smallest shark in the world. This tiny one has one of the longest names: *tsuranagakobitozame,* Japanese for "dwarf shark with a long face." The luminous shark, a twenty-incher that glows green in the dark, is another oddity, found in warm waters of the Pacific, Atlantic, and Indian oceans.

The goblin shark, which lives in the Indian Ocean, has a weird-looking head. Its jaws are like an alligator, and its forehead juts out like a sharp stick.

Angel sharks have wings, which are really wide fins. They seem to fly through the water. The angel is also called monk shark, a strange name for a shark that looks more like a devil. There are about ten known species, inhabiting waters all over the world. In ancient Rome, people used angel shark flesh to cure pimples. If it could really do this, it would deserve the name "angel."

THE RAYS,
ODD-LOOKING
COUSINS

No account of weird-looking sharks would be complete without including their close cousins the rays. They are an odd-looking bunch.

Like sharks, they have no bones, and they have the same kind of gills and teeth. They also eat the same kind of food. Some of them look so much like queer sharks that only scientists can tell whether the fish is a ray or a shark. One way they tell is by the location of the gills. If the gill slits are on the side of the head, the fish may be a shark; if the gill slits are underneath the head, the fish may be classified as a ray. The guitarfish, a ray, looks almost the same as the angel shark. And the sawfish, another ray, has a look-alike in the saw shark.

Called winged sharks, rays are often described as transformed sharks whose bodies have become flat and whose fins have grown large. Their long, skinny tails look like whips.

If you ever saw a manta ray, also called devilfish, you would never forget it. A manta can weigh up to a ton and measure twenty-four feet from fin to fin. Mantas have been

Above: the sawfish, with its long nose.
Right: unborn sting rays,
with their whip-like tails.

flapping around the sea for millions of years. They are the giant bats of the ocean, eaten by sharks but feared by most other creatures.

The stingray uses its tail to slash and stab its victim. The tail is a dagger with barbs like fishhooks along its shaft. And there is a sac of poison at the end of the tail. Should a stingray lose its valuable tail, it grows a new one.

Poison, slashing, stabbing, and biting are among the ray's methods of hunting for dinner. Add electricity to the list. There is an electric ray that kills fish with an electric charge. It is only a foot long, but it can shock anyone.

Skates are a kind of ray. Most of them are small, kite-shaped creatures with sharp noses and long, skinny tails. They flap around in cold and warm waters all over the world. There are over three hundred kinds of skates and rays. Luckily they usually don't attack people.

Learning More about Sharks

In their search for more knowledge about sharks, scientists have set up laboratories on land and at the bottom of the sea. Jacques Cousteau built several buildings in the Red Sea. A team of **oceanauts** spent four weeks at Starfish House, one of Cousteau's undersea laboratories. Antishark cages with alarm signals were connected to Starfish House. For added protection, each oceanaut carried a shark billy. This is a pole with nails at the end to poke sharks and send them away. During their undersea explorations the oceanauts watched sharks pass them by, seeming not to notice them. At other times the sharks fled. Sometimes they zoomed in to attack, bending the metal bars of the cages, trying to get to the human bait inside. No one can predict what sharks will do. We still don't know too much about why and when a shark will attack.

To learn about sharks, scientists **tag** them. Boats go out on special tagging expeditions, and either the scientists shoot plastic tags into the sharks' fins, or skin divers tag the sharks with special spears, while exploring. The

Sometimes an attack is the best defense, as this diver shows, frightening away a tiger shark.

A biologist tags a blue shark during a research cruise.

(63)

tag has instructions in five languages. It asks the person who catches the shark to return the tag by mail, to describe the shark, and say where and when it was caught. Scientists have been getting thousands of these tags from all over the world.

Tagging tells us about migrations — where sharks travel. We have learned that one blue shark swam three thousand miles from New York to Africa. We also know that a mass meeting of sharks takes place every December off the coast of lower California. That's where the gray whales come to breed, and sharks go there to eat the gray whales. The big mystery is how sharks know when and where the whales breed.

Scientists, testing the sharks' intelligence, have been able to train them. A baby shark proved to be so smart that it was invited to the Royal Palace in Japan in 1965.

This baby shark learned to ring a bell for its dinner. It received its schooling from Dr. Eugenie Clark, at the Mote Marine Laboratory in Florida. It was one of the many sharks living in a large pond, where they were being tested to find out how fast they learn and how well they see.

Every day two different targets were put in the pond. When a shark hit its head against one target, a bell rang

A shark of this type — a lemon shark — took part in Dr. Clark's Florida training experiments.

and food was thrown down as a reward. The other target had no dinner bell.

Sharks learned to see the difference between the targets. After several weeks they hit only the dinner bell target. The prize pupil was a baby nurse shark who learned twice as fast as the grown-ups.

Crown Prince Akihito of Japan heard about this remarkable young shark and invited it to the palace. Carrying the young shark in a plastic bag of water the size of a hatbox, Dr. Clark flew to Tokyo.

The little shark was housed in the palace. When it felt at home swimming in front of the prince, Dr. Clark placed two targets in the water. The baby shark rang the dinner bell at once. A royal servant used chopsticks to feed it lobster from a platter fit for an emperor.

Dr. Clark and other scientists are trying to find a shark repellent — any object, sound, or smell that would keep sharks away. Perhaps some day a wristband will be worn that sends out sounds sharks hate. Or a chemical will be thrown into the water to make the area shark-safe. Undersea explorers and people in life rafts need shark repellents.

There are fewer than one hundred recorded shark attacks a year in the whole world, and fewer than half of the victims have been killed. However, thousands of bad auto accidents take place every day in the United States. The most dangerous part about going swimming is driving to the beach. Bulls, snakes, and spiders kill more people than do sharks. You have more chance of being hit by lightning than you have of being bitten by a shark.

The shark is not an evil, bloodthirsty, man-eating monster. It's an amazing creature that hunts and eats to survive. Not fear but interest should make us want to know more about sharks, rulers of their world, the sea.

Glossary

Barbels. Fleshy whiskers that help fish feel and taste food in the water around them.

Cannibal. A member of a species that eats another member of the same species.

Cartilage. An elastic gristlelike substance that is a substitute for bone.

Claspers. Sharks' male sex organs.

Dermal denticles. Teeth on the shark's skin.

Digest. To change or break up food, within the body, into a form that can be used by the body.

Enamel. The hard outer layer of teeth.

Feeding frenzy. The behavior of groups of sharks that, while attacking prey, attack each other and try to eat anything in the area.

Fins. Paddlelike organs attached to fishes that help them swim, steer, and keep their balance.

Gill rakers. Stiff sticks of cartilage that keep food in the shark's mouth and stop food entering the gills.

Gills. Fishes' breathing organs. Sharks have five to seven pairs.

Lateral line. A line along the head and sides of fishes that feels water pressure.

Oceanauts. Undersea explorers.

Pit organs. Sense organs in the shark's skin that enable it to feel.

Plankton. Floating masses of tiny plant and animal matter.

Pressure waves. Changes in water pressure caused by nearby objects or other fishes.

Primitive. Being like, or only slightly changed from, the earliest kinds in history.

Pups. Newborn and young sharks.

Shagreen. Leather made from shark skin.

Sounding. Going straight down in the water instead of swimming down at a slant.

Species. A related biological group of any living things having the same qualities.

Sperm. Male fluid that fertilizes eggs.

Tagging. Attaching plastic or metal tags to fish, using a dart gun or spear. The tag has an address and instructions for anyone who catches or finds the fish.

Tendrils. Sticky, threadlike strings that act as anchors for eggs laid in water.

Vertebrate. Any animal with a backbone or spinal column.

Bibliography

Brown, Theo. *Sharks: The Silent Savages.* Boston: Little Brown, 1973.

Budker, Paul. *The Life of the Shark.* New York: Columbia, 1971.

Clark, Eugenie. *The Lady and the Sharks.* New York: Harper and Row, 1969.

Cousteau, Jacques and Philippe. *The Shark: Splendid Savage of the Sea.* New York: Doubleday, 1970.

Cropp, Ben. *Shark Hunters.* New York: Macmillan, 1969.

Cook, Joseph, and Weisner, William. *The Nightmare World of the Shark.* New York: Dodd Mead, 1968.

Helm, Thomas. *Shark!* New York: Dodd Mead, 1961.

Lineaweaver, Thomas, and Backus, Richard. *The Natural History of Sharks.* Philadelphia: Lippincott, 1970.

Matthiessen, Peter. *Blue Meridian: The Search for the Great White Shark.* New York: Random House, 1971.

McCormach, Harold, and Allen, Tom. *Shadows in the Sea.* Philadelphia: Chilton, 1963.

Index

About the Author

Rhoda Blumberg lives on a farm near Yorktown Heights, New York. Traveler, deep-sea fisherwoman, tennis player, and book collector, she has written interviews for CBS radio programs; magazine articles on criminals, daredevils, millionaires, and scientists; books on a dozen foreign countries, and *Fire Fighters* (A First Book), published by Franklin Watts. Last year she hooked a very large nurse shark off the Florida Keys. When it surfaced, her husband took the rod and reeled the shark near enough to the boat for her to photograph it. Then it was let go.